THIS NOTEBOOK BELONGS TO..

CONTACT..

See our range of fine, illustrated books, ebooks, notebooks and art calendars:
www.flametreepublishing.com

This is a **FLAME TREE NOTEBOOK**
Published and © copyright 2018 Flame Tree Publishing Ltd

FTPE11 • 978-1-78755-217-3

Edge detail is created by Flame Tree Studio and based on an artwork by
Sunny Designs/Shutterstock.com

FLAME TREE PUBLISHING | The Art of Fine Gifts
6 Melbray Mews, London SW6 3NS, United Kingdom